Original title:
Marriage in the Modern Age

Copyright © 2024 Swan Charm
All rights reserved.

Author: Olivia Orav
ISBN HARDBACK: 978-9916-89-184-1
ISBN PAPERBACK: 978-9916-89-185-8
ISBN EBOOK: 978-9916-89-186-5

Unplugged Promises

In the quiet dusk we stand,
Promises whispered, hand in hand.
The world fades, the noise goes down,
In this moment, love is found.

Eyes closed tight, we breathe in time,
Every heartbeat, a perfect rhyme.
No screens, no texts, just you and me,
In silence, our souls roam free.

The stars above begin to glow,
In this stillness, our secrets flow.
Each gentle touch, a binding thread,
In the night, our words are said.

Days will pass, seasons will change,
Yet our hearts will not rearrange.
With every sunset, we renew,
These unplugged promises, forever true.

Heartbeats in the Cloud

Floating high in skies of blue,
Heartbeats echo, pure and true.
Digital whispers on soft wings,
In the cloud, our love still sings.

Connected souls across the miles,
Each message brings a thousand smiles.
Through the ethers, our thoughts collide,
In this space, there's nowhere to hide.

We share our dreams and quiet fears,
In pixelated love, we shed tears.
With every tap, a spark ignites,
Heartbeats dancing through the nights.

Though distance lies beneath our feet,
In the cloud, our hearts will meet.
These moments crafted, heart-defined,
In every text, your hand in mine.

Two Souls, One Screen

In a world framed within a glance,
Two souls find their second chance.
With every swipe, a story told,
In glowing light, our love unfolds.

Late-night chats and morning texts,
In each word, our hearts are vexed.
We share our thoughts with laughter's grace,
Finding warmth in cyberspace.

Virtual hugs across the line,
In every pixel, love will shine.
Two souls connected, one single thread,
In this screen, our dreams are spread.

Moments captured, always near,
Through the wires, I bring you here.
In every pause, a silent prayer,
Two souls entwined, no need for care.

Whispered I Do's in the Era of WiFi

Beneath the glow of evening light,
We gather close, hearts taking flight.
With every whisper, truths unfold,
In bytes of love, our vows are told.

WiFi signals dance in the air,
As promises flow without a care.
Streaming love on this special day,
In virtual realms, we find our way.

Laughter shared through screens so bright,
In every moment, joy ignites.
"I do"s echoed, soft and clear,
A love that grows, year by year.

In this era, we make our stand,
Hand in hand, we dream and plan.
Whispers linger, love will bind,
In the digital space, our hearts entwined.

The Language of Togetherness in Truncated Text

In whispers soft, we type
Our hearts aligned, side by side.
Each word a pulse, a spark
Bridges built in pixel tide.

Emojis dance, a smile's grace,
A single heart, we both embrace.
Through screens we weave our fate,
In silence loud, we celebrate.

With every ping, joy ignites,
Conversations flow through night lights.
A world apart, yet so near,
In this text, our love is clear.

Distance fades, connection grows,
In fragments, love forever flows.
Together in this digital space,
A love that time cannot erase.

So let our voices intertwine,
With every message, your heart is mine.
In words condensed, we find our way,
Together, come what may.

Emblems of Affection in a Snap.

A fleeting moment, captured bright,
A snapshot sealed in soft twilight.
In laughter shared, our eyes entwined,
Emblems of love, we both find.

With every click, memories bloom,
Framed in light, dispelling gloom.
A whispering breeze through tangled hair,
In frozen time, the world laid bare.

Details fade, but feelings last,
In every picture, shadows cast.
In frames we live, each smile a gift,
Snapshots of love, our spirits lift.

Captured warmth on cloudy days,
In every snap, a million ways.
Emblems of joy, our story told,
In vibrant colors, love unfolds.

So click away, dear, my beloved,
In these moments, we are covenanted.
With each photo, life's embrace,
Emblems of affection, time cannot erase.

Eternal Vows in Digital Light

Under the glow of a lit screen,
We cast our dreams, pure and keen.
With every promise, truth takes flight,
Eternal vows in this digital light.

In pixels bright, our hearts align,
As fingers tap, your hand in mine.
A world transformed by words we share,
In circuits bound, a love so rare.

With distance marked, yet close at heart,
In every message, we're never apart.
This bond we forge will only thrive,
In the rhythm of data, we are alive.

From silence to sound, our love will grow,
In vibrant streams, emotions flow.
For deep within this coded night,
Eternal vows in digital light.

So here we stand, against the tide,
In binary code, I take this ride.
Forever cherished, forever bright,
Our love shines true in digital light.

Love's Algorithm: A Binary Bond

In zeros and ones, our hearts begin,
A logic dance of passion's spin.
Through tangled code, we find a way,
Love's algorithm guides our play.

Each heartbeat clicks, a data pulse,
In this system, a strong impulse.
Through signals sent, our souls collide,
In binary worlds, we won't divide.

Formulas crafted in whispered dreams,
In every byte, love softly gleams.
A structure built on trust and grace,
In lines of code, we find our place.

With each update, our bond expands,
In virtual hands, no fate withstands.
This language spoken in shared reply,
Love's algorithm will never die.

Together we map this endless sea,
In calculations, you and me.
For destined codes will meet and bond,
In the vast expanse of love's beyond.

Synaptic Sparks

In the quiet hum of night,
Thoughts collide, a flash of light.
Neurons dance, a wild spree,
Feel the rush, come set me free.

Whispers roam, electric tides,
In your eyes, the truth resides.
A universe in every glance,
Together we create the chance.

Memories weave like threads of gold,
Stories shared, our hands unfold.
As sparks ignite in silent air,
Two souls meet without a care.

The world around begins to fade,
In the light, our fears betrayed.
Moments linger, hearts entwined,
In this space, our love defined.

As dawn breaks, the colors blend,
With every heartbeat, we transcend.
Together in this cosmic play,
Synaptic sparks will lead the way.

A Blueprint for Tomorrow's Love

On the canvas of our dreams,
Drafting plans that burst at seams.
Each gesture, a careful stroke,
A bond that words will not invoke.

Laying bricks of trust and grace,
Building moments we embrace.
With laughter echoing in the halls,
Our hearts rise, never fall.

Colors blend, a vibrant scheme,
Sketches drawn of love's grand theme.
Blueprints made with passion's fire,
In the heart, our true desire.

As we nurture this design,
Crafting futures, yours and mine.
Through shadows, light, and stormy weather,
We reshape worlds that last forever.

In a blueprint, love takes flight,
Guided by our shared insight.
Each day a page, in ink anew,
Together, we will see it through.

Love Unplugged

In a world of glowing screens,
Let's find beauty in the seams.
Put away the noise and haste,
Taste the moments that we waste.

Holding hands beneath the stars,
No more echoes, just ours.
Silence speaks where words may fail,
In each breath, our souls exhale.

No notifications, just the night,
Lost in you, my guiding light.
Every heartbeat, pure and true,
Our essence thrives in all we do.

With every touch, the sparks renew,
A timeless dance, just me and you.
Here we stand, unplugged, alive,
In this moment, we truly thrive.

In nature's arms, we've found our place,
Love's embrace, a gentle grace.
Together, we roam this quiet land,
In love unplugged, forever stand.

The Essence of Togetherness in Pixels

Captured moments in a frame,
Pixels dance, they know our name.
Click and pause, a memory stored,
In this digital love, we're adored.

Every image tells a tale,
In vibrant hues, emotions sail.
Side by side in screens aglow,
Together through both high and low.

Zoom in close, let colors blend,
In each shot, we find a friend.
Perfect moments, smiles so bright,
Framing love in purest light.

Filters fade, but truth remains,
In this realm, we break the chains.
Through every click, our hearts align,
In a world of pixels, you are mine.

So let's treasure this montage shared,
Laughing loud, always prepared.
In every snapshot, love persists,
The essence of us, blissfully kissed.

The Filtered Union

In shadows cast by screens we meet,
A symphony of hearts discreet.
With every shared and whispered thread,
We weave a tale, our spirits fed.

Through distant lands, our voices soar,
In filtered light, we find much more.
Each pixel bridges time and space,
Together, we embrace this place.

Yet in this dance of light and sound,
Real bonds form where love is found.
Our laughter echoes in the void,
In every pixel, joy employed.

From fleeting glances to deep sighs,
In filtered moments, truth still lies.
Though screens may separate the day,
In hearts and minds, we find our way.

So let us pledge, through screens we create,
To cherish bonds that love will sate.
In this filtered world, we rise and shine,
United spirit, yours and mine.

Ties That Bind in a Virtual World

In a realm where avatars play,
Connections bloom in the light of day.
Through glowing screens, we reach and touch,
In this world, we find so much.

With every chat and every swipe,
We trace the lines of dreams and hype.
A bond created, though not face-to-face,
In this digital dance, we find our place.

Yet storms may gather in the night,
And doubts may shadow digital light.
Still, hearts ignite with every word,
In whispered realms, our hopes are stirred.

Though worlds apart, our spirits blend,
In pixels, we find a steadfast friend.
Through laughter and tears, we will endure,
These ties that bind, forever pure.

So let us navigate this virtual sea,
Bound together, just you and me.
For in this space where dreams unfold,
Our story sparkles, bright and bold.

Love Anchored in Realities

Beneath the stars, our hearts entwined,
In whispered hopes, our souls aligned.
Where moments linger, shadows play,
In real embrace, we greet the day.

Through trials faced and journeys shared,
In every heartbeat, love declared.
The world may spin, but here we stand,
With open hearts, we hold each hand.

With colors bright and laughter free,
Our dreams take flight, just you and me.
The weight of life, a gentle guide,
In synchronized steps, we will glide.

Though storms may rage and skies may cry,
Together, we'll never say goodbye.
With anchors set in truth and grace,
We find our home in love's embrace.

So let the world around us change,
In love's embrace, we'll stay unchanged.
For every moment, joy revealed,
In anchored hearts, our fate is sealed.

Promises Beyond Pixels

Within the glow of distant screens,
We weave together fragile dreams.
In every click, a vow we make,
To build a bond that will not break.

With whispered words in midnight's glow,
Through tides of time, our feelings flow.
In every message, trust unfolds,
A treasure born, more precious than gold.

But life beyond the pixel's glow,
Holds truths that only lovers know.
In every heartbeat, every sigh,
The essence of love will never die.

So hand in hand, we stride ahead,
With promises of all that's said.
In worlds apart, we'll find our way,
Together, brightening the day.

With every step in our journeywide,
We'll cherish love, our faithful guide.
For in this realm, both real and grand,
Our promises bloom, forever planned.

The Instant Connection

In a crowded room, we found our way,
A glance exchanged, a dance to sway.
Moments frozen in a fleeting gaze,
A spark ignites, in a digital haze.

Words typed softly, hearts laid bare,
Each keystroke a sign that we're aware.
Laughs shared late, through the glowing screen,
A bond formed quick, but fiercely keen.

Fingers fumble, as we reach for hands,
In this world of light, our longing stands.
Tonight we'll weave our stories tight,
In the instant connection, everything feels right.

No space between, just us entwined,
A union brought forth by hearts aligned.
In every heartbeat, a whispered plea,
This instant connection, eternally free.

A Union of Notifications

Ding! A message, my heart takes flight,
Each ping and buzz, igniting the night.
Our world revolves around screens so bright,
In a union of notifications, love's in sight.

Buzzing reminders, of moments shared,
Each scroll and tap shows how much we've cared.
Threads of laughter, connections so bold,
In every alert, a new story unfolds.

Digital whispers that hold us tight,
In this vast web, our spirits take flight.
Together we rise with each loving tone,
In a union of notifications, we're never alone.

Under stars, we pause and reflect,
The beauty of love in every direct.
Through screens and beats, our truths collide,
In this union of notifications, forever our guide.

Swipe Right for Forever

In a world of choices, so many to see,
With a simple gesture, you came to be.
A swiping motion, a chance we take,
Swipe right for forever, let hearts awake.

Profiles crafted with care and delight,
Each image a treasure, shining so bright.
With every right swipe, possibilities grow,
In this search for love, the best seeds we sow.

Conversations blossom, each word a design,
A connection that's fueled by a force divine.
Together we laugh, and together we dream,
Swipe right for forever, like a flowing stream.

Dates filled with magic, as we find our place,
In this digital dance, we float and embrace.
With each passing moment, we cherish the lore,
Swipe right for forever, hearts longing for more.

Hearts in the Age of Automation

In the hum of machines, we still can feel,
Hearts beating softly, a primal appeal.
Through code and circuits, we seek the spark,
In the age of automation, we must leave our mark.

Eyes that wander beyond the screen,
In every heartbeat, a chance to dream.
With breaths entwined, the world fades away,
As we dance together, both night and day.

Connections sparked through electric threads,
Laughter shared in what the future spreads.
Emotions coded in lines of light,
Hearts in the age of automation, burning bright.

Together we navigate this tangled maze,
Finding solace in each other's gaze.
Amidst the chaos, love finds its way,
In hearts in the age of automation, we'll stay.

Coexisting in a Digital Patchwork

In pixels we find our voices,
A chorus of distant hearts,
We weave through wires and screens,
Creating art that never parts.

Our worlds collide in circuits,
United by glowing light,
Fragments of lives interlace,
In the tapestry of night.

Digital dreams take their shape,
Fleeting as shadows cast,
Yet deep connections linger,
In the echoes of the past.

We craft new realms together,
As code gives way to care,
In this patchwork of existence,
Love flourishes unaware.

So here we stand, connected,
In a dance of ones and zeroes,
Bridging gaps with compassion,
In this landscape of heroes.

Stories Written in the Code

Beneath the lines of syntax,
Whispers of dreams take flight,
In each command and series,
Lives unfold into the night.

A tapestry of data,
In binary we confide,
With every click and keystroke,
We share what's deep inside.

From algorithms born,
Memories drift like mist,
Encoding our emotions,
In the programs that persist.

Together we create pathways,
In the labyrinth of thought,
Navigating through the silence,
In the worlds we have wrought.

So let our stories linger,
Written in strands of light,
For in the realm of coding,
Love's narrative ignites.

Love's New Landscape

In the garden of the virtual,
Hearts blossom like spring,
The landscape shifts with yearning,
In the solace that we bring.

Through messages and laughter,
We cultivate the ties,
With every heartfelt moment,
We uncover hidden skies.

Pixels paint our passions,
In shades both bold and bright,
Navigating through the shadows,
In the glow of digital light.

Our love knows no borders,
A map drawn out in dreams,
Exploring realms together,
In whispered data streams.

Hence, we journey onward,
Hand in virtual hand,
In love's new landscape thriving,
Across this endless land.

Connections Beyond the Horizon

A sun that sets in pixels,
Spills colors of the day,
We reach beyond the skyline,
In hopes that words will stay.

Across the seas of silence,
Voices beckon and call,
In the vastness of connection,
We rise together, stand tall.

Threads that bind us tightly,
Resilience in the storm,
In the face of distance,
Our hearts take on new form.

We map out our emotions,
On the canvas of the night,
Finding joy in synchrony,
In the dance of shared light.

With every dawn, a promise,
Of bonds that will not sway,
For connections beyond the horizon,
Guide us on our way.

Love in the Era of Swipe

Fingers dance on glowing screens,
Hopes wrapped up in silent dreams.
Each swipe a chance, a fleeting spark,
Yet hearts still yearn for deeper dark.

Endless profiles, faces rare,
Yet none can match your tender stare.
In this quicksand, connections fade,
Yet here I stand, unafraid.

Ghosts of dating, laughter once shared,
Amidst the chaos, love declared.
Infinity rolls beneath our feet,
In fleeting moments, we find our beat.

Cross the miles with a single tap,
Finding solace in our digital map.
Through pixels bright, our souls entwined,
In every story, a love defined.

So let us stand, against the tide,
In every swipe, let love abide.
Authentic hearts through screens will find,
A lasting bond, forever kind.

Hearts Aligned in the Cloud

Floating high on data streams,
Where every love is wrapped in dreams.
Connected worlds, beneath the stars,
Our hearts aligned, despite the scars.

Messages whisper, a gentle cheer,
In each response, I feel you near.
Video calls under moonlit skies,
In a digital realm, our spirits rise.

Though miles apart, the bond is strong,
In this vast web, we belong.
Together we laugh, share hopes, and fears,
In the cloud, we dry our tears.

Love's encryption, secure and tight,
Sending warmth through the endless night.
In every pixel, a story blooms,
Hearts aligned, chasing love's tunes.

So let's embrace, when the world seems cold,
A love like this is worth more than gold.
In our shared space, we'll always find,
Together forever, heart and mind.

Moments Captured in Feeds

Snapshots of laughter, smiles so bright,
A glimpse of joy, shared day and night.
In timelines woven, we build our tale,
Each moment cherished, like a holy grail.

Scrolling through memories, soft and sweet,
Every glance a love note, bittersweet.
Filters may fade, but feelings stay true,
In a sea of faces, I see you.

Hashtags echo the love we share,
Pictures paint stories beyond compare.
In every click, a memory caught,
In the gallery of hearts, you're what I've sought.

Capturing seconds, yet feeling so vast,
All our tomorrows, built on the past.
In digital frames, where moments don't flee,
With every post, it's you and me.

So let's create, in each shared space,
A timeline of love, our special place.
For every feed holds what we deem,
A life of love, a vivid dream.

The New Rituals of Togetherness

Cafés buzzing, but screens aglow,
Together apart, in a trendy show.
Hands meet a cup, hearts in a race,
Finding warmth in this strange space.

Evenings spent in shared delight,
Gifts wrapped up in digital light.
Conversations flow through Wi-Fi's lane,
Bonding over joy and shared pain.

Time spent streaming shows anew,
Laughter echoing in every cue.
Building moments in this hybrid place,
Togetherness framed in a virtual embrace.

Weekend plans through pixels reside,
Navigating life with love as our guide.
While distance stretches, hearts remain true,
In ritual and spark, it's me and you.

So lift your glass to moments we share,
In laughter and love, we find care.
In this new world, our hearts will align,
The rituals of love, forever divine.

Love's Modern Mosaic

In fleeting glances, hearts collide,
A tapestry of souls untied.
Each laugh a thread, each sigh a seam,
In love's embrace, we dare to dream.

Digital whispers, shadows cast,
Moments cherished, but never passed.
With every swipe, we seek the true,
Within the chaos, I find you.

Fragments stitched with tender care,
In crowded rooms, it's us who dare.
Among the noise, we find our song,
A melody where we belong.

With every word, a spark ignites,
Guiding us through the starry nights.
Together we weave our shared delight,
In love's mosaic, pure and bright.

Reflections in the Age of Oversharing

In pixels bright, we share our lives,
But truths get lost, where noise derives.
Beneath the filters, hearts remain,
Hiding the joy, the hurt, the pain.

Notifications buzz, but who's there?
In silent moments, do we care?
A world defined by likes and views,
Yet crave connection, deep and true.

In streams of data, we reveal,
The fabric of what we conceal.
Are we more than what we show?
In quiet corners, love can grow.

Reflecting on what really matters,
As golden moments turn to tatters.
Let's pause and cherish every spark,
Beyond the screens, find light in dark.

A Script for Two

In whispered words, our story starts,
With gentle touches, linking hearts.
We pen the lines, our world unfolds,
Together, in the warmth, we mold.

In laughter shared and sorrow borne,
Through every tear, our bond is worn.
A dance of love, a waltz so fine,
In every step, your hand in mine.

With chapters written, dreams embraced,
In every pause, our hope interlaced.
The script unfolds, with twists and turns,
In every page, our spirit burns.

Let's write the scenes of softest grace,
Where every glance holds a warm embrace.
In moonlit nights and dawn's first hue,
Our love, the script, forever new.

Harmonizing Hearts in a Fast-Paced World

In rush of life, we seek the calm,
Amidst the chaos, find the balm.
Each heartbeat sings a silent tune,
Two souls in rhythm, under the moon.

Through crowded streets, we walk as one,
Finding beauty in the run.
A laugh, a touch, a fleeting glance,
Together in this daring dance.

As time ticks on, we breathe in deep,
In moments sweet, our secrets keep.
With every second that slips away,
We treasure love in the light of day.

In harmony, our spirits blend,
A symphony that knows no end.
Through storms and sun, our hearts align,
In the fast-paced world, your hand in mine.

Love's New Grammar

In whispers soft, we find our words,
A language born of shared glances.
With every text, the heart's unheard,
We weave our dreams in silent dances.

Through screens we touch, connect and drift,
Emojis bridge the great divide.
In frames of light, our spirits lift,
Love's new grammar, where hearts confide.

The stories spin in pixels bright,
Each message holds a world of care.
We write our vows in fading light,
Two souls entwined in electric air.

In threaded chats, our lives unfold,
Each heartbeat captured in a line.
In cyberspace, more than mere code,
Our love, a story so divine.

At midnight hours, we dream and share,
In midnight screens, our secrets flow.
A timeless bond forged in the air,
Our hearts connected, ebb and glow.

Home: A Shared URL

In every room, your laughter lingers,
A web of warmth that draws me near.
Together, we are woven singers,
A melody for hearts to hear.

Shared memories locked within these walls,
A URL to moments past.
In every echo, love recalls,
A haven where our dreams hold fast.

Windows wide, the world outside,
Yet here in arms, we find our place.
A shared URL, where hopes abide,
In every touch, a soft embrace.

With every dawn, we build anew,
Our stories brush the skies so bright.
Two hearts entwined, as morning dew,
A home that blooms with endless light.

Together, we craft a peaceful zone,
In laughter's glow, fears disappear.
This shared URL, our hearts have grown,
A sanctuary, forever here.

Real Life, Real Hearts

In crowded rooms, our eyes collide,
A spark ignites, reality shines.
With every heartbeat, love's the guide,
In life's wild dance, your hand in mine.

We face the storms, the sun's warm rays,
In laughter's echo, tears we share.
Each winding path, through varied days,
We find our truth in moments rare.

In whispered dreams beneath the stars,
We chase the dawn, our spirits free.
In every scar, we've stitched our scars,
Together, we write our own story.

The simple joys, a picnic spread,
In tranquil parks, our worries fade.
With every glance, our words unsaid,
In real life love, our vows are laid.

As seasons change, our roots go deep,
We blossom bright, through thick and thin.
In hearts entwined, our promises keep,
This real life love, forever begins.

Love Letters in the Digital Age

Through screens, we share our hearts laid bare,
With every click, a love anew.
In pixels bright, we voice our care,
Love letters sent through virtual blue.

The morning light on empty screens,
A waiting soul for words to write.
In every line, a promise gleans,
Two lovers lost in soft delight.

With hashtags bright, our hearts will soar,
In every post, the world will know.
Through subtle texts, we crave for more,
A dance of love in ebb and flow.

In every scroll, a memory unfolds,
Snap a moment, capture the day.
With every share, our story told,
Love letters, now in bright display.

And when the night cloaks all in gray,
We pen our dreams on haunted screens.
In this new world, we find our way,
Love letters written between the scenes.

From Likes to Lifetimes

In a world of taps and swipes,
We found connection, pure and bright.
Through screens we shared our dreams,
Transforming likes into life's streams.

Moments captured, pixels aligned,
Hearts entwined, our fate combined.
From strangers to lovers we grew,
In a digital dance, love was true.

Through late-night calls and messages sent,
Our souls connected, time well spent.
Every like held a secret sigh,
In this virtual space, we learned to fly.

With every post, our story unfurls,
In the labyrinth of this modern world.
From fleeting glances to lasting vows,
Together forever, we'll show the hows.

So here we stand, side by side,
From likes to lifetimes, there's no need to hide.
In this digital age, love's flame ignites,
A journey bound by heart's delights.

Crafting a Home in Hyperlinks

In a realm where pixels loom,
We built a heart, our digital room.
With every click, a memory made,
Crafting a home where love won't fade.

Hyperlinks connect our laughter's sound,
In this space, true joy is found.
Every shared link a story told,
In cyberspace, our hearts unfold.

Through virtual halls our dreams do roam,
In every chat, we find our home.
Interwoven tales in every phrase,
Crafting a world where we blaze.

With GIFs and memes, we paint our skies,
A tapestry woven, where spirit flies.
In this pixelated embrace we find,
The essence of love, uniquely designed.

So here we dwell, in code and light,
Creating a home, a perfect sight.
In each hyperlink, our love will grow,
A sanctuary built, where hearts overflow.

Time Travelers in Love

Through ages past, we journeyed far,
Time travelers beneath the same star.
With whispers soft, we crossed the years,
In every moment, we faced our fears.

From ancient days to futures bright,
Our love's a beacon, a guiding light.
In paradoxes, we intertwine,
Timeless hearts that align just fine.

With every tick of time's embrace,
We share a glance in every place.
Future's echo in present's tear,
Together we conquer time's wild sphere.

Time bends for us, a sweet ballet,
With every heartbeat, we find our way.
In every second, our souls ignite,
Time travelers in love's pure flight.

So let the clocks tick on, we'll soar,
In every timeline, we'll explore.
With love as our map and dreams as our guide,
In the fabric of time, we will abide.

A Symphony of Shared Screens

In quiet rooms, we play our parts,
A symphony of synced-up hearts.
With shared screens, we touch and see,
Creating harmony, you and me.

Every pixel sings a tune,
In the glow of the evening moon.
As laughter echoes through the wires,
We weave a web of sweet desires.

Through whispered words and silent sighs,
Our love reflects in soulful eyes.
In every frame, our stories blend,
A melody that will never end.

With every call, a tender note,
In this concert, we freely float.
Together in rhythm, we find our place,
A symphony of love, a warm embrace.

So let the music of us resound,
In every moment, beauty found.
Through shared screens, we write our song,
In this duet, where we belong.

Pixels and Heartbeats

In a world of glowing screens,
Where silence speaks in bright machines,
Connections made in fleeting times,
We share our dreams in pixel rhymes.

A heartbeat felt through wires' hum,
In every pulse, a story spun.
Across the miles, our voices blend,
In digital dawn, where friendships mend.

From shadows where our spirits thrive,
We paint the moments, keep love alive.
With every click, a bond defined,
In every frame, a path entwined.

Our laughter echoes, loud and clear,
In bits and bytes, we're always near.
Through every storm, we share the light,
In pixels bright, our hearts take flight.

So let us weave this tapestry,
With every thread, a memory.
In this realm where dreams ignite,
We'll dance together, day and night.

Union of the Unseen

In realms where shadows softly blend,
We find the ties that never end.
A touch of spirit, soft and bright,
In whispers shared beneath the night.

Our paths unseen, yet always near,
A bond that flourishes sincere.
With every thought, our voices soar,
In silent strength, forever more.

Across the waves of time and space,
We search for warmth, for love's embrace.
In every heartbeat, pulse of grace,
United souls in this vast place.

Through unseen threads,   ,
    Connecting paths where hope begins.
A world revealed in silent glow,
In unity, our power flows.

So let us cherish what we find,
The unseen union, hearts aligned.
Together, we will transcend the veils,
In bonds unbroken, love prevails.

The Journey Beyond the Swipe

With every swipe, we seek and yearn,
Exploring corners, watch fires burn.
In fleeting moments, stories grow,
A journey crafted, seed we sow.

Through pixels' dance, our lives unfold,
In whispered tales, our hearts are told.
Adventure beckons, bold and true,
Each swipe a step towards something new.

Lost in a labyrinth of the mind,
Where echoes linger, truth we find.
Beyond the screen, the world awaits,
In every heartbeat, fate creates.

So take a breath, let courage rise,
Beyond the swipe, the dream complies.
In every glance, a universe,
Our journey calls, let's break the curse.

Together, we'll explore the night,
Unravel paths and chase the light.
For in this world of endless tries,
The journey blooms before our eyes.

Connected Souls

In crowded rooms, we feel alone,
Yet in our hearts, a truth is known.
For every glance, a spark ignites,
In silent realms, our love unites.

Through every word and whispered sigh,
We find the strength to reach the sky.
Connected souls, we dance as one,
In every shadow, light begun.

With open arms, we share our fears,
In laughter's echo, dry our tears.
Together, we embrace the night,
In harmony, we spark the light.

Through woven tales, we break the wall,
With every rise, we challenge fall.
In every moment, dreams unfurl,
In connected souls, we change the world.

So let us cherish every thread,
With love that reaches where we're led.
In this connection, sights unseen,
We find our place in realms serene.

Distant Stars

In the nights of endless skies,
We trace the paths where starlight lies.
Distant dreams that softly call,
In cosmic dance, a fate for all.

With every twinkle, tales unfold,
Of whispered wishes, brave and bold.
In galaxies where secrets swim,
Our hearts align, on fate's bright rim.

Through cosmic winds, we send our hopes,
Across the vast, where spirit copes.
In every spark, a journey glows,
A tapestry of cosmic flows.

Unraveling threads of time and space,
In distant stars, we seek our place.
For every dream that lights the night,
A universe of pure delight.

So let us reach for dreams afar,
With courage bound, we'll touch a star.
In every heartbeat, we're not far,
For love connects us, just like stars.

Forever in a Text

Words typed and sent, forever remain,
In digital whispers, love's sweet refrain.
A heart emoji speaks louder than time,
In pixelated realms, our souls do climb.

Midnight confessions, a tap on the screen,
The warmth of your voice in a message unseen.
Longing delivered in moments so small,
Forever inscribed in the ether, our call.

Each notification pulses with light,
Your name on my phone feels just so right.
A distance bridged by the keys that we press,
In a world wrapped in text, I find my happiness.

In moments of silence, your words echo clear,
Through laughter and tears, our bond becomes near.
From simple exchanges, our story takes flight,
Forever in text, our love burns bright.

As pixels dance, a new realm we find,
In each little message, hearts intertwined.
Forever in a text, our love will renew,
In every sweet letter, I'll cherish you too.

Foundations of a Life Shared

Two hearts entwined, we lay the first stone,
Building a home where love can be known.
Brick by brick, through laughter and pain,
Foundations of life formed in sun and rain.

Shared dreams painted on canvases wide,
In colors of hope, we take every stride.
Moments of joy, like stars in the night,
Together we shine, a beautiful light.

Side by side, through the ebb and the tide,
With trust as our anchor, nothing can hide.
In whispers of promises, futures create,
Foundations of love, our hearts navigate.

Each laughter rings true, each sorrow we share,
Hands clasped together, life's burdens we bear.
On this path we tread, with faith we will climb,
Building a life, one moment at a time.

In the tapestry woven, our stories unite,
Celebrating love, day turning to night.
Foundations of life, in each other's embrace,
A bond that will solidify, never erase.

Virtual Altars and Real Feelings

In glowing screens, our hearts find a place,
Virtual altars where we seek solace.
In GIFs and emojis, our laughter runs free,
Yet real are the feelings that live deep in me.

Pixels divided, yet nothing can sever,
The bond that we share, it feels like forever.
With just a few taps, emotions ignite,
In this digital haven, everything feels right.

Late-night confessions, confounding the night,
We walk hand in hand, though out of sight.
The space may be virtual, but love is so true,
In pixels and words, my heart's still with you.

Through screens we connect, in moments so rare,
Every shared story, a truth laid bare.
In this world of code, our spirits are free,
Virtual altars built on sincerity.

In laughter and tears, we truly connect,
Real feelings bloom, for our hearts intersect.
Though miles may divide, love knows no bounds,
In virtual altars, our joy resounds.

The Art of Compromise in Connectivity

In the web we weave, we learn to align,
Through give and through take, our hearts intertwine.
Waves of the past, they shift and they sway,
In the dance of connection, we find our own way.

Balancing dreams, both yours and my own,
In the silence of moments, understanding is grown.
With open hearts, we navigate the unknown,
The art of compromise, in love we've been shown.

The lines that we draw may sometimes blur,
Yet together in wisdom, our vision will stir.
Each push and each pull, a rhythm to learn,
As we nurture our bond, in passion we'll burn.

In laughter and trials, our patience shines bright,
Through storms and calm seas, we find our own light.
With hands clasped together, no challenge too steep,
In compromise lived, our promises keep.

For love isn't simple; it's crafted with care,
In hearts that connect, a journey we share.
The art of being one, through lessons we glean,
In connectivity's dance, our souls are serene.

Heartbeats Through Screens

In the glow of our devices,
We share our dreams and fears.
Emojis dance like fireflies,
Connecting hearts through tears.

Every ping ignites a spark,
Across the miles, we find a way.
A silent bond that carries on,
In the night, until the day.

Fingers tap on glassy seas,
Unraveling thoughts so deep.
In the rhythm of our beats,
These moments we shall keep.

Screens may fade, but love will glow,
In every message sent.
Heartbeats echo, strong and true,
A love that won't relent.

So let the pixels flicker bright,
In this realm where we reside.
Through screens, our souls entwine,
Together, we will glide.

Vows Under Neon Lights

Beneath the urban glow, we stand,
With hearts aglow and hands entwined.
Promises whispered close and soft,
In neon dreams, our love defined.

The city hums, a pulsing beat,
As laughter dances with the night.
In every glance, a world anew,
Two souls, drawn close with sheer delight.

Every vow a timeless thread,
Woven through the city's heart.
In the warmth of this bright embrace,
We craft our lives, a work of art.

As the stars blend with the signs,
We find our way, together bold.
In the shimmer of the streets we roam,
Our tale of love will unfold.

So let the neon light the path,
As we journey, hand in hand.
In this electric symphony,
We'll always understand.

Love in the Digital Whisper

In whispers shared on screens so bright,
We weave our hopes with tender care.
Words like soft feathers, take their flight,
Soaring high in digital air.

With every message sent at dawn,
A little piece of us remains.
In virtual realms, our love is drawn,
Binding hearts with gentle chains.

Facetime calls, a glance, a smile,
Bridging gaps that time creates.
In pixels, we traverse each mile,
Love blossoms as it resonates.

A thousand tokens, sweet and rare,
For every heartbeat yet to come.
In whispers, we lay our hearts bare,
Creating echoes, soft and numb.

So here's to love in fleeting texts,
In this space, we find our way.
Beyond the noise, our hearts connect,
Together, we forever stay.

Promises Beyond Pixels

Beyond the screen, we make our vows,
In silent spaces filled with light.
Promises whispered, soft and low,
Building dreams that shine so bright.

With every click, another tale,
Each moment shared, a thread we weave.
Though distance stretches like a veil,
In love, we learn to truly believe.

Timely texts, in joy and woe,
Binding us through day and night.
In the heartbeats that we know,
Promises linger, holding tight.

A future drawn in softest hues,
As pixels dance in kindred glee.
In every moment, we choose,
To anchor love in you and me.

So let the world outside unfold,
While stories bloom in cyberspace.
Together, we defy the cold,
Our promises, a warm embrace.

Knots Tied in Streaming Signals

Frayed threads of old connections,
Glimmers in a digital dawn.
Whispers lost in pixel oceans,
New ties formed before the morn.

Chasing echoes through the wires,
Hearts pulsing in electric streams.
Messages woven like desires,
Dreams and hopes blaze in our dreams.

Sparks ignite with every heartbeat,
Tangled in the virtual chase.
Fields of data, bittersweet,
We search for warmth in endless space.

Yet beneath the glowing faces,
Yearnings crave a simpler time.
Bind our souls in real embraces,
Unraveling these knots sublime.

The future calls, the past recedes,
In fleeting moments, love will grow.
Through streaming signals, planted seeds,
A garden blooms, a vibrant show.

The Dance of Modern Hearts

Tonight, we sway in neon lights,
Rhythms pulse through sparks and shades.
Every breath, our souls ignite,
In this techno-fueled serenade.

Glances shared across the space,
No words needed, just a spark.
Fingers brushing, a sweet embrace,
In this moment, we leave our mark.

Step by step, we spin with grace,
Time dissolves in music's flow.
In the chaos, we find our place,
Two modern hearts begin to glow.

Lost in beats and vibrant dreams,
Together we create new tunes.
As the world fades, nothing seems,
To match the magic of our moons.

The dance of love, it knows no bounds,
Through every twist, our spirits soar.
In silent whispers, joy abounds,
Together, forever, we explore.

Rekindling Fire in a Click

Fingers hover over keys,
Old flames flicker, memories soar.
In the glow, a warmth we seize,
Rekindled hearts that yearn for more.

A simple message stirs the night,
Soft laughter dances through the air.
With every click, the sparks ignite,
Reviving moments that we share.

Lost connections now arise,
In the comfort of our screens.
Digital love, a sweet surprise,
Bringing back what might have been.

Through pixels and electric hopes,
We bridge the gap of distant years.
Finding solace, learning to cope,
Rekindling fire, facing fears.

Every click unravels the past,
While forging paths that intertwine.
In this dance, our love will last,
Bound in warmth, our hearts align.

Embracing Change

Winds of change sweep through the trees,
Carrying whispers from afar.
We gather strength beneath the breeze,
Learning lessons from each scar.

Steps uncharted, hearts set free,
A journey forward, fears laid bare.
Through every twist, we see clearly,
In the unknown, love finds its share.

With open arms, we greet the dawn,
Surrendering to time's embrace.
In every end, a spark is drawn,
Every moment holds a trace.

Reflections of what used to be,
Guide our steps on this new path.
Each trial faced, a victory,
In embracing change, we find our math.

Together, we rise, bold and bright,
Creating stories in the light.
Hand in hand, we'll take that leap,
In change, our dreams begin to seep.

Cherishing Rituals

In small moments, rituals bloom,
Morning tea shared side by side.
Quiet laughter dispels all gloom,
In cherished space, our hearts reside.

Evening walks beneath the stars,
Counting blessings, hand in hand.
Simple joys erase the scars,
In these small things, love will stand.

Seasons shift, yet we remain,
Traditions hold us, anchor tight.
Through changing tides, we feel no pain,
In every shadow, there's a light.

Stories woven through the years,
Each thread binds us, strong and true.
In laughter, love, and sometimes tears,
These sacred rites, our bonds renew.

Together, we craft our own lore,
In the heart of all we've found.
Cherishing rituals, we explore,
Life's tapestry, forever bound.

Embracing the Hybrid Union

In quiet spaces where worlds collide,
Traditions meld with the tech we guide.
A dance of past and future bright,
In harmony, we find our light.

Bridging gaps with open hearts,
New paths pave, as old depart.
Holding hands across the lines,
Unity in all it defines.

Voices merge, a symphony plays,
Echoes of long-forgotten days.
Weaving stories, we share our truth,
In this fusion, we find our youth.

With every challenge, we grow wise,
In the hybrid, potential lies.
Together we forge a brand-new way,
For every night leads to day.

Through every doubt, we will stand tall,
In our union, we conquer all.
Each step forward, hand in hand,
Embracing love across the land.

Gleaning Truths from 280 Characters

A brief tweet, a world unveiled,
In concise words, our hearts are hailed.
Characters dance and stories bloom,
In short phrases, we find the room.

Messages pulse with vibrant life,
Sharing joys and also strife.
In snippets shared across the air,
Connections weave, our thoughts laid bare.

From distant lands, a voice aligns,
In simple lines, a truth defines.
Within the limit, wisdom grows,
A tapestry of highs and lows.

We capture moments, fleeting quick,
In lovely streams, the heartbeats tick.
With each character, we share a dream,
In this vast space, we learn to beam.

Amidst the noise, clarity shines,
Echoing across the digital lines.
In brevity, we feel the weight,
Gleaning truths, we transcend fate.

The Intersection of Old and New

In ancient folds, whispers reside,
While progress surges with the tide.
Crafting futures from the past,
In every moment, legacies cast.

Old tales told in modern ways,
Building bridges across the maze.
The wisdom of yesterday guides,
As innovation alongside abides.

From stone to screen, a journey made,
In shadows cast, our dreams won't fade.
Rekindling flames of culture bright,
A fusion born in shared insight.

Every epoch, lessons flow,
In every heart, the echoes grow.
With open minds, we seek to blend,
In this union, we find a friend.

The beauty lies in what we keep,
As memories from ashes leap.
At this confluence, we create,
A vibrant world that resonates.

Hearts Bridged by Technology

Across the miles, our spirits soar,
In coded beats, we open doors.
With every click, a bond ignites,
In digital realms, love takes flight.

Vibrant screens, reflections bright,
Connecting souls with endless light.
Each message sends a tender care,
In virtual whispers, we find air.

Tech weaves dreams, a shared embrace,
In pixels formed, we find our place.
Through networks wide, we send our love,
In this bridge, we rise above.

From distant lands, familiar faces,
Creating spaces in new places.
Though miles apart, we feel so near,
In bytes and bits, we persevere.

With every heartbeat, connections thrive,
In cyberspace, we feel alive.
Hearts united in this great dance,
Together we take our timeless chance.

Love's New Compass

In the glow of the evening light,
Hearts dance close, holding tight.
With every glance, the world feels right,
Together we forge our love's flight.

Maps of dreams drawn in the sand,
Navigating hand in hand.
Through every storm, we bravely stand,
Trust is our true, guiding brand.

Stars above in a velvet sky,
Whispers soft, a gentle sigh.
In this moment, we dare to fly,
Love's new compass, you and I.

Journeys shared, paths intertwine,
Moments caught, forever mine.
For every hill, a love divine,
Together, hearts and souls align.

Through the seasons, we will grow,
In joy, in pain, we ebb and flow.
With each heartbeat, I will show,
My love for you, a steady glow.

Conversations Across Continents

Miles apart, yet close we feel,
Through screens aglow, our thoughts reveal.
Shared laughter, dreams, and wounds we heal,
In words exchanged, life's joy we steal.

Nations wide, yet hearts unite,
Voices echo through the night.
Cultural tales take brilliant flight,
In each shared moment, pure delight.

From cities bright to quiet farms,
Conversations weave with loving charms.
Every story holds its arms,
Embracing all with its warm balms.

Time zones shift, yet we find time,
To share our lives, to speak in rhyme.
Language flows like sweetest chime,
In connections built, we find the prime.

Across the globe, our dreams align,
In every chat, a secret sign.
No borders here, no need to pine,
For friendship's bond, forever fine.

The Story We Share Online

With every post, a piece is told,
In pixels bright, our lives unfold.
Moments captured, memories bold,
In virtual realms, connections gold.

Likes and shares bring smiles and tears,
In comments, laughter fills the years.
We find our tribe, among our peers,
In shared stories, we calm our fears.

From morning light to evening's glow,
We navigate this digital flow.
In every story, love will grow,
United through what we both know.

Behind each screen, a heart's embrace,
Faces smiling, leaving a trace.
In every laugh, in every face,
We share a bond, time can't erase.

So let us scroll and always find,
In threads and links, a love designed.
For every word, a chance to bind,
The story shared, forever kind.

Bonds Forged in the Ether

In quiet moments, silence speaks,
Echoes of love, in whispers, peaks.
Through wires and waves, our bond unique,
In digital skies, our hearts do seek.

Voices travel, crossing the void,
In laughter shared, no need for ploy.
With every text, a heart deployed,
Connections strong, never destroyed.

As stars align, our paths converge,
In every chat, our souls emerge.
Through trials faced, through love's surge,
Together we stand, let fears purge.

The ether hums with stories bright,
In every moment, pure delight.
Bonds unbreakable shine like light,
In this vast world, with you, I fight.

So here we write our tale anew,
In every word, there's me and you.
Forever forged in skies so blue,
Our hearts entwined, deeply true.

Uniting Souls in Online Spaces

In quiet rooms we gather round,
With screens aglow, our hearts unbound.
Each click a spark, a whispered tale,
In digital realms, our dreams set sail.

No distance too great, no night too long,
In virtual warmth, we all belong.
Together we laugh, together we cry,
In the web of connection, we learn to fly.

Through chat and video, we share our days,
In pixels and bytes, love finds its ways.
With every message, bridges we build,
In this online space, our hearts are thrilled.

Bonds Forged in Virtual Embrace

Screens flicker brightly, hearts start to mend,
In a world of pixels, we find a friend.
Threads woven tightly through laughter and tears,
In this warm embrace, we conquer our fears.

Together we forge what distance can't break,
In each conversation, new pathways we make.
With emojis and memes, we share our delight,
In our virtual haven, we shine so bright.

Connection surges, electric and clear,
In whispered moments, we draw ever near.
With every shared story, our spirits ignite,
In bonds forged in pixels, we soar to new heights.

A Dance of Text and Time

Words paint a canvas, our thoughts intertwine,
In the rhythm of typing, hearts start to chime.
Each message a step in our delicate waltz,
A dance through the storms, a truth that exalts.

Time may keep ticking, yet here we remain,
Crafting our moments through joy and through pain.
In the lull of each silence, our hearts still speak,
In the dance of the text, we find what we seek.

With every notification, excitement anew,
In this virtual realm, it's just me and you.
We twirl through the hours, lost in this play,
In a dance of our own, we drift and we sway.

Love Letters in a Click

With every keystroke, a letter arrives,
Carrying whispers, where love truly thrives.
In this world of ones, in this world of zeros,
We craft our heartbeats, our digital heroes.

Moments unfold with a simple 'ping',
In this swift ballet, we discover our wing.
Each word a petal, each line a sweet song,
In messages sent, we feel we belong.

Through screens we find solace, our hearts intertwine,
In the poetry of clicks, our souls brightly shine.
Love letters whispered in bits and in bytes,
In this modern embrace, our love takes flight.

Echoes of a Shared Life

In the quiet whispers of the night,
Memories dance within our sight.
Every laugh, a soft refrain,
Echoes linger, joy and pain.

Fingers trace the distant stars,
Mapping dreams across the bars.
In our hearts, we keep the light,
Guiding us through shadowed plight.

Time may fade, but moments stay,
Locked in cherished, secret sway.
With every heartbeat, love expands,
Binding us with gentle hands.

Through the storms and sunny days,
We find strength in countless ways.
Together we will face the tide,
In this bond, we take great stride.

A lifetime etched in every glance,
In this love, we found our chance.
Through the echoes, we'll survive,
In each other's arms, we thrive.

Threads of Love in a Digital Fabric

Pixels blend in vibrant hues,
Every click, a love we choose.
In a world where screens divide,
Our affection cannot hide.

Messages like woven threads,
Crossing paths where courage spreads.
Hearts connect through distant miles,
Bringing forth our truest smiles.

Each tweet and post a bridge we span,
Crafting moments, hand in hand.
Through the chaos, we create,
A tapestry that won't abate.

In this pixelated dance, we roam,
Finding comfort far from home.
In the quiet of the night,
Love expands, a guiding light.

Together in this vast embrace,
Every heartbeat finds its place.
In our digital embrace we grow,
Threads of love in vibrant flow.

Virtual Kisses, Real Embraces

In a world of ones and zeroes,
Love transcends, it gently flows.
Virtual kisses sent with care,
Creating warmth, a bond we share.

When the distance draws us thin,
Reaching out, our hearts begin.
Each typed word, a tender touch,
In these moments, we feel so much.

Screens flicker, but we remain,
Guarding hearts against the pain.
In dreams that whisper sweet and low,
Real embraces help us grow.

Time zones clash, yet love won't wane,
Every heartache, joy, and strain.
Navigating through the night,
Together, we will find the light.

So let the pixels pave our way,
With every dawn, a new display.
In this realm of hopes and grace,
We find our love, our sacred space.

Navigating Love's New Map

In the digital expanse we roam,
Finding paths, we carve our home.
Heartbeats sync across the miles,
Lost in laughter, found in smiles.

Through the layers of code we share,
A journey led by love and care.
Circles drawn on every screen,
Mapping dreams yet to be seen.

With each message, a step we take,
In this dance, our hearts awake.
Navigating twists and turns,
In this love, our passion burns.

Guided by stars both near and far,
Together, you're my guiding star.
Let's chart a course, no turning back,
On love's ever-changing track.

In the end, what matters clear,
Is the bond we hold so dear.
Through the maps of love, we thrive,
Together, forever, we survive.

Sharing Tomorrow, Today

In whispers soft we share our dreams,
With hopes that shine like twilight beams.
Each moment cherished, hearts in sync,
We build a bridge, we dare to think.

With hands entwined, we plant the seeds,
Of tomorrows born from present needs.
Time flows like rivers deep and wide,
Together, love, we'll turn the tide.

In laughter shared, the woes all fade,
With every choice, a path we've made.
Tomorrow's light, a gentle guide,
With you, my love, I'll always bide.

Through every storm, we find our way,
In shared tomorrows, come what may.
From fleeting glances to tender sighs,
We'll paint our world with endless skies.

So here's to today, a canvas bright,
Let love be bold, let dreams ignite.
Together we'll carve our place in time,
In love's sweet dance, a perfect rhyme.

The Ties That Bind: A Digital Tale

In pixels bright, our stories blend,
A web of dreams where messages send.
Through screens we touch, through bytes we share,
Connections forged, we find each other there.

A meme, a post, a virtual cheer,
In digital realms, we hold you near.
With every click, a heartbeat grows,
A tapestry woven as the world knows.

In chats and threads, our laughter rings,
Through coded lines, the joy it brings.
A bond unbroken by distance or time,
With every word, we find our rhyme.

In virtual hugs, the comfort flows,
In pixels and bytes, our love still grows.
Though screens divide, our hearts align,
In this digital tale, love's designed.

From every share to every trend,
The ties that bind, they never end.
In this vast space, we make our mark,
With every spark, we light the dark.

A Love Ledger in Binary Code

In ones and zeros, our love is stored,
A ledger carved, forever adored.
Each byte a kiss, each bit a touch,
In digital dreams, we mean so much.

From timeless whispers in silent night,
To data streams that feel so right.
With algorithms penned in heart and soul,
A passionate script that makes us whole.

In circuits deep, our stories live,
With every share, we gladly give.
A syntax sweet, we write our tale,
In love's great code, we'll never fail.

Through firewalls high and networks wide,
Our love endures, it will not hide.
In every login, our hearts entwined,
A beautiful bond, uniquely designed.

With data threads, we stroll along,
In binary beauty, we find our song.
Together we dance in this endless flow,
In a love ledger, we'll always glow.

Captured Moments, Lasting Impressions

In frames of gold, the moments stand,
Each click a story, a touch of hand.
Captured glances, a fleeting spark,
In memories bright, we leave our mark.

With laughter loud, and tears we share,
In every picture, love's essence there.
Through seasons change, in time's embrace,
We hold forever in a captured space.

From sunlit days to starry nights,
The laughter lingers, the heart ignites.
In every snapshot, a world in view,
With moments cherished, I cherish you.

As years go by, the story flows,
In every chapter, our garden grows.
With lasting impressions, we'll sketch anew,
In the art of life, it's me and you.

So here we stand, in frames we trust,
With love immortal, in memories we must.
In every smile, in every tear,
Captured moments, forever dear.

Digital Footprints of Forever

In silent webs where we align,
Our paths entwined, a thread so fine.
Each click, each smile, a mark we share,
In virtual realms, we show we care.

Through screens we touch, our hopes ignite,
In distant lands, we find our light.
Through glowing screens, our voices sound,
A bond that grows, though miles surround.

Memories stored in bits and bytes,
In this vast space, our love ignites.
Like shadows cast, our essence stays,
In echoes of our shared displays.

With every post, a piece is sent,
In this digital, our hearts are bent.
Threads of our lives, loosely entwined,
In cyberspace, our souls aligned.

As time moves on, the world may change,
Yet love persists, it feels so strange.
Through every storm, we hold our ground,
In digital footprints, forever found.

Together in the Half-Light

In gentle dusk, where shadows play,
We find our words, we drift away.
Whispers soft in muted glow,
Together in this ebb and flow.

With heartbeats shared, like whispered sighs,
In half-light's warmth, no need for lies.
Together we stand, hand in hand,
As twilight's brush paints the land.

The world around us fades to gray,
Yet in this moment, here we stay.
A silent promise in our gaze,
Together lost in evening's haze.

Time slows down in this embrace,
In half-light's grasp, we find our place.
No need for lights, our spark is bright,
In this cocoon, we share the night.

As stars emerge and night unfolds,
We weave our dreams, our stories told.
In whispers soft, our hearts unite,
Together always in the half-light.

Pixels of Affection

In every pixel, love takes flight,
A canvas painted, pure delight.
Colors blend, our laughter shines,
In digital frames, our heart entwines.

With every message, warmth we share,
In every emoji, a silent care.
Like stars above in midnight skies,
Our affection glimmers, never dies.

Through filters bright and frames so neat,
We capture moments, bittersweet.
In every snapshot, a memory gleams,
Pixels of love, stitched from dreams.

Swipe to the left, a gentle touch,
In this bright world, we matter much.
Our stories told in vibrant hues,
In every click, our love renews.

As time moves on, our tales grow vast,
In pixels' glow, we hold the past.
With every post, we write our song,
In this dance of pixels, we belong.

The Modern Matrimonial Quilt

In threads of love, we stitch our fate,
A modern quilt, it resonates.
Each patch a story, rich and bold,
In every seam, our lives unfold.

With colors bright, our hopes entwined,
In laughter shared, our hearts aligned.
Together woven, strong and tight,
In this fabric, we find our light.

Through joy and sorrow, each piece tells,
Of whispered dreams and echoed bells.
A tapestry of hands and hearts,
In this quilt, our journey starts.

As seasons change and time persists,
We gather warmth in love's sweet kiss.
Each patch a moment, stitched with care,
In this quilt of life, we always share.

With every stitch, our bond grows strong,
In every corner, we belong.
A modern quilt, both soft and true,
In love's embrace, we'll see it through.

Discovering Us in a Disrupted World

In the chaos, we find our way,
Seeking light in shadows' play.
Hands reach out, hearts ignite,
Together we rise, ready to fight.

Voices blend in the night's embrace,
Finding comfort in our space.
Through the noise, our laughter rings,
In this storm, love's joy brings.

Moments stolen, time compressed,
In our chaos, we are blessed.
Every heartbeat, every sigh,
In this world, we learn to fly.

Glimmers of hope, shining bright,
Guiding us through darkest night.
With each step, we redefine,
In this journey, you're mine.

With open hearts, we weave a tale,
Navigating love's vast gale.
Enduring change, we're never lost,
In our bond, we bear the cost.

Infinite Scroll

Fingers dance on glowing screens,
Chasing dreams through digital seams.
Time slips by with every click,
Lost in feeds, we grow so thick.

Moments captured, stories shared,
Yet in stillness, we are scared.
Faces fade, connections wane,
In the scroll, our hearts feel pain.

Endless scrolling, fleeting time,
Lonely hearts in a crowded rhyme.
Finding meaning, searching deep,
In the noise, do we still keep?

Eyes glued tight, yet minds will roam,
Hunting solace, far from home.
In the rush, we seek the real,
A deeper bond, a truer feel.

Pause for breath, take a chance,
Rediscover life's sweet dance.
In the silence, find your core,
Life's much more than an open door.

Finite Time

Ticking clocks remind us all,
Moments fade, like leaves that fall.
Cherish each breath that we take,
In this fleeting time we make.

Love's embrace in a knowing glance,
Together we weave, together we dance.
Time is precious, slipping fast,
What we hold is built to last.

With every call, with every sigh,
We grasp at stars in the night sky.
In laughter shared and dreams we hold,
We write our story, brave and bold.

Time may race, but love will stay,
Guiding our hearts along the way.
In these moments, both small and great,
We find our joy, we find our fate.

Together we shine, light the way,
Infinite love, come what may.
For in this dance of day and night,
Time is ours, and love is light.

Threads of Connection

In the fabric of our lives,
Invisible threads, our spirit thrives.
Stitch by stitch, we weave the ties,
In each other, find the skies.

Through laughter shared and tears we shed,
In every word, love is wed.
From heart to heart, the echoes flow,
In these connections, we learn to grow.

Moments crafted in the silent night,
In whispered dreams, we take flight.
Holding on to what is true,
In every thread, I'm stitched to you.

Find the strength in unity,
In diversity, we find beauty.
With open arms, we face the tide,
In these threads, together we stride.

Resilient spirit as one we stand,
Binding tight, hand in hand.
In the tapestry of life, we'll find,
Love's true essence, pure and blind.

Love's Compass in the Algorithms

In a world of coded fates,
Algorithms set the gates.
Yet love defies the cold design,
A compass true, by heart aligned.

Through data streams, our hearts can roam,
Navigating paths, we seek our home.
With every pulse, every sign,
In the chaos, your hand is mine.

Numbers dance, but feelings bloom,
Amidst the bytes, we break the gloom.
Love's warm glow, a guiding star,
In the cyber sea, you're never far.

In the metrics, find our ground,
Our laughter echoes, love resounds.
With every challenge, we rise anew,
Together forging what is true.

So let the world compute and track,
Our hearts will always find their way back.
In every loop and every turn,
With love's compass, forever we yearn.

Ties That Transcend Timezones

Across the seas, our voices soar,
In whispered dreams, we seek for more.
Through endless nights and blazing suns,
Our hearts entwined, the journey runs.

With stars above that guide our way,
In every night, you'll find my sway.
A love that grows with every call,
No distance large can break our thrall.

Embrace the miles; let love ignite,
Through time and space, we hold on tight.
Moments shared, though far apart,
You are my light; you are my heart.

From dawn to dusk, our laughter streams,
We bridge the gap with hopeful dreams.
No clock can bind what we create,
In every code, we celebrate.

United still, we mend the seams,
In every text, we stitch our dreams.
A tapestry of love and time,
Together always, in our rhyme.

Echoes of I Do in Cyberspace

In virtual halls, our vows resound,
As echoes of love spread all around.
A click, a swipe, our hearts in sync,
With every pulse, we stop and think.

Streaming love in a pixel glow,
Through hearts entwined, our spirits flow.
Each word a promise, a solemn pledge,
In cyberspace, we'll build our edge.

With every video, our souls take flight,
From dusk till dawn, we hold on tight.
In all the bits, our love is clear,
As cyberspace pulls you near.

A dance of light on glowing screens,
In every chat, we share our dreams.
Through wires and waves, our voices find,
In love's embrace, we are aligned.

Together we stand, though worlds apart,
In every byte, you have my heart.
With every echo, our vows take shape,
In cyberspace, our lives escape.

United by Algorithms

In coded lines, our paths align,
A world of hearts that intertwine.
With every click and every scroll,
We find a way to touch the soul.

Through data streams, our love is spun,
A dance of joy where algorithms run.
With every swipe, the sparks connect,
In digital realms, we feel the effect.

We map our dreams in binary code,
Each secret shared, our love exploded.
In every search, your smile remains,
Our love transcends the giving chains.

United by streams of text and light,
In every post, you feel so right.
Together we stand, a digital link,
In this vast world, our hearts are inked.

Through ones and zeroes, our voices blend,
In every heartbeat, you're my friend.
With algorithms, we craft our fate,
In love's embrace, we cultivate.

Traditional Meets Trending

Old tales told with modern flair,
In harmony, we build a pair.
With roots deep in the past we stand,
Embracing now, we hand in hand.

A timeless dance with steps renewed,
With every rhythm, we are imbued.
We honor love in every way,
With classic charms that brightly sway.

Through ancient words and trending ways,
We weave our story, night and days.
With every laugh, the past takes flight,
In every moment, we find the light.

A fusion of hearts, both old and new,
Together crafting something true.
In every glance, a world reborn,
With love that's rich, we greet each morn.

Through cherished customs and fresh designs,
We bridge the gap by love's designs.
In every heartbeat, we combine,
For traditional meets trending, divine.

Timeless Affection in Timed Chats

In fleeting moments, we share our hearts,
Words float between us, where time departs.
Connection blooms in a digital space,
Timeless affection, no need to chase.

With every message, a warmth ignites,
Laughter and stories light up the nights.
Though distance may linger, our bond is tight,
In timed chats, love takes wondrous flight.

Our lives intertwine in this virtual thread,
Echoes of laughter, the things that were said.
Even in separation, we don't feel alone,
In the rhythm of typing, our hearts have grown.

So let's treasure these moments, short yet profound,
In written exchanges, true love is found.
Through pixels and screens, affection flows,
In limitless spaces, our connection grows.

As time ticks softly, we cherish the now,
In chats that unite us, we take our vow.
For timeless affection in these fleeting talks,
Is the heartbeat of love, as our journey walks.

Celebrating Uniqueness in Tandem

In a world of colors, we find our place,
Two hearts in tandem, a beautiful grace.
Unique in our rhythms, yet perfectly aligned,
Together we flourish, joy intertwined.

With every quirk, we embrace the light,
Dancing to music that feels just right.
Your laughter's a melody I hold so dear,
Celebrating uniqueness, we conquer fear.

Hand in hand, we traverse the unknown,
Through valleys of doubt, we have grown.
In the tapestry woven, each thread is a prize,
We celebrate differences, and rise to the skies.

As stars above sparkle, just like our dreams,
Two souls in harmony, or so it seems.
Together we create an extraordinary tale,
In this wonderful journey, our hearts will prevail.

So here's to the moments when we shine bright,
In the dance of our lives, we find pure delight.
Celebrating uniqueness, each step we take,
In tandem, forever, no matter the break.

Hearts That Navigate the Noise

In a world full of chatter, we find our way,
Two hearts that navigate, come what may.
Through the clamor and chaos, we stand side by side,
In the symphony of life, love is our guide.

Amidst all the noise, your voice is a song,
Resonating deeply, where we both belong.
With each whispered word, our fears go away,
Together we flourish, come night or day.

We cherish the silence when the world gets loud,
In our quiet moments, we feel so proud.
With every heartbeat, our connection grows,
In harmony's embrace, love always knows.

Through storms and through struggles, we face with grace,
Hearts navigating together, our shared space.
In the melody of life, we write our own tune,
With every adventure, like stars in the moon.

So let's dance to the rhythm of what we create,
Two souls intertwined, an unbreakable fate.
In a world full of noise, we're a sweet refrain,
Together forever, through joy and through pain.

Rhyme and Reason in a Digital World

In this digital world, we find our rhyme,
Crafting connections, defying time.
With every keystroke, a verse is born,
In pixels and screens, we weather the storm.

Through laughter and tears, we share our tales,
Navigating heartbreaks, where comfort prevails.
Each message a line in our growing script,
In the dance of the digital, we boldly equip.

With wisdom and wonder, we paint our dreams,
In a canvas of moments, a life bursting at the seams.
Reason and passion, together they weave,
In this digital realm, we dare to believe.

So let's create stanzas that echo the heart,
In a world of connections, we play our part.
With rhyme and with reason, our story unfolds,
In the beauty of words, our truth is told.

As we journey through bytes, our spirits take flight,
In the glow of the screens, everything feels right.
For in this race of technology and time,
We flourish together, our voices in rhyme.

Banners of Belonging in Binary

In coded whispers, we unite,
Lines of love in pixels bright.
Each connection, a thread that binds,
Banners of belonging, in shared designs.

In circuits woven, hearts will glow,
Through wires and waves, our feelings flow.
Binary dreams in colors swirled,
Together we rise, a brand new world.

In virtual realms, we start to dance,
Echoes of laughter, a joyful chance.
Among the data clouds, we soar,
Claiming our space, forevermore.

With every signal, we dive deep,
Sowing the love we long to keep.
Our story told in hashtags bright,
Banners of belonging, a guiding light.

Pixels shift, but souls remain,
Through every loss, through every gain.
Together we'll stitch a tale so true,
In binary beats, I'm here with you.

Interwoven Paths of Progress

Step by step, we carve the way,
With hopes that guide, come what may.
In tangled trails, we find our strength,
Interwoven paths at every length.

Through stormy nights and sunlit days,
We share our dreams in countless ways.
Each twist and turn, a lesson learned,
In the heart's furnace, courage burned.

Together we venture, side by side,
In unity's embrace, we abide.
Every milestone, a shared delight,
Interwoven paths into the light.

With hands held tight, we reach for stars,
Navigating life, despite the scars.
In every challenge, growth we see,
Interwoven paths, you and me.

So let us forge a future bright,
With every step, our spirits light.
Together we rise, our dreams confess,
In interwoven paths of progress.

Love's Playlist in a Streamed World

In melodies that softly play,
Our hearts entwined, come what may.
Each note a memory, sweet and kind,
Love's playlist streaming, beautifully designed.

Through whispered lyrics, stories flow,
Fueled by rhythms only we know.
In every chord, our dreams are spun,
Together in harmony, we're never done.

From golden oldies to brand new sounds,
In the dance of life, love abounds.
Every song, a chapter shared,
In love's playlist, we are prepared.

As echoes linger in the air,
We weave our hopes, our tender care.
Through highs and lows, we sing along,
In love's playlist, where we belong.

So press play, let the music guide,
In each heartbeat, side by side.
For in this world, where dreams are swirled,
Love's playlist shines, a streamed world.

Unscripted Moments in Filtered Frames

In captured glances, time stands still,
Unscripted moments, a spontaneous thrill.
Through filtered frames, our laughter rings,
In the art of life, joy brightly clings.

Each scene unfolds, a tale untold,
In vibrant colors, life unfolds.
With every snapshot, we cherish the now,
In the beauty of chaos, we take our vow.

Embracing the flaws, the truth appears,
In candid smiles and joyful tears.
Through every snapshot, memories bloom,
Unscripted moments, dispelling gloom.

The frames may filter, but love's the core,
In every heartbeat, we long for more.
Capturing life, as we take our aim,
Unscripted moments, forever the same.

So here's to the pauses, the breaths we take,
In every instant, new paths we make.
Together we'll wander, endless and free,
In unscripted moments, just you and me.

Building Dreams with Bytes

In the glow of screens, we play,
Crafting visions, night and day.
With each click, our dreams take flight,
Pixels dance in virtual light.

Lines of code, like threads we weave,
In this world, we dream and believe.
Building bridges with every line,
A tapestry of futures divine.

From shadows cast by digital streams,
We carve our plans, we shape our themes.
Together we rise, through data's light,
In the realm of hope, we unite.

So let the bytes ignite our hearts,
As we craft our roles, play our parts.
With every dream, we lay the stone,
Building a world where love is grown.

In the ether, our dreams align,
Through endless code, your hand in mine.
For in this dance of bytes we trust,
Our digital dreams are gold, not dust.

Heartstrings in the Cyber Space

In a world where echoes roam,
We find each other, far from home.
Through screens, our laughter flies,
Painting love beneath the skies.

Typing words, a love profound,
In every message, hearts unbound.
Across the void, we share our fears,
With every byte, we dry our tears.

Heartbeats sync in virtual streams,
In this space, we chase our dreams.
Through tangled wires, our souls embrace,
Finding warmth in cyber space.

In whispers caught in digital winds,
We create a world where love begins.
Through pixels pure, we intertwine,
In every heartbeat, the stars align.

So let the world fade far away,
In this haven, we choose to stay.
For love knows not what distance means,
Together forever, in cyber dreams.

In the Canvas of Connectivity

Each click a brushstroke, bright and bold,
On the canvas where our tales unfold.
Through the wires, colors collide,
In this realm, our dreams abide.

Swirling hues of hope and delight,
Painting connections, shining bright.
With every heartbeat, we share our art,
A masterpiece birthed from the heart.

In the gallery of souls intertwined,
Every moment a treasure designed.
Through the pixels, our stories flow,
In connectivity, we learn and grow.

Each frame a memory, cherished and dear,
Brushes of laughter, paints of fear.
In this canvas, life's wonders gleam,
Creating a world woven with dreams.

So stand with me in this vibrant space,
Together we'll sketch our own embrace.
In the tapestry of time and place,
We find our home, our sacred grace.

Rewriting Our Love Story

In the margins of forgotten pages,
We find the love that never ages.
With every word, we start anew,
Rewriting dreams, just me and you.

Chapter by chapter, we pen our fate,
Through twists and turns, we navigate.
Each moment an ink drop on the line,
Crafting a tale where hearts intertwine.

From the ashes of doubt and fear,
Rising like phoenixes, we draw near.
With each glance, a plot twist appears,
Together we conquer, beyond our years.

The ink may smudge, but love remains,
In every paragraph, joy and pains.
With whispered secrets and daring dreams,
Our love story glows, bursting at the seams.

So take my hand, let's turn the page,
In this adventure, we're free from cage.
For in the words we write each day,
Our love's the ink that lights the way.

Milton Keynes UK
Ingram Content Group UK Ltd.
UKHW021207261024
450281UK00007B/94